The Classic Cake Baking Cookbook

Best Cake Recipes from Scratch

Table of Content

Introduction

If you are looking for cake recipes for beginners, you have to try this book. A homemade cake is definitely tastier than the store bought one. But many people believe that making a cake at home is difficult. The best thing about homemade cake is that you can add any flavour of your choice to suit your palate. If you get the quantities right, the cake will rise, be fluffy and taste delicious. Cakes are simply the best. A perfectly baked moist cake is one of life's simple pleasures. Baking cakes at home can be just as fun as eating them as long as you have the right recipes! This book is going to give you **The Best Cake Baking Recipes** in the World!

Hummingbird Bakery marshmallow cupcakes recipe

Ingredients

- 120g plain flour
- 140g caster sugar
- 1½ tsp baking powder
- a pinch of salt
- 45g unsalted butter, at room temperature
- 120ml whole milk
- 1 egg
- ¼ tsp vanilla extract
- 12 medium pink marshmallows
- 200g mini marshmallows

For The Frosting:

- 1 quantity vanilla frosting
- Edible glitter, to decorate

- A 12-hole cupcake tray, lined with paper cases

Method

- To make this **cupcake recipe,** preheat the oven to 170°C (325°F) gas 3.
- Put the flour, sugar, baking powder, salt and butter in a freestanding electric mixer with a paddle attachment (or use a handheld electric whisk) and beat on slow speed until you get a sandy consistency and everything is combined. Gradually pour in half the milk and beat until the milk is just incorporated.
- Whisk the egg, vanilla extract and remaining milk together in a separate bowl for a few seconds, then pour into the flour mixture and continue beating until just incorporated (scrape any unmixed ingredients from the side of the bowl with a rubber spatula). Continue mixing for a couple more minutes until the mixture is smooth. Do not overmix.
- Spoon the mixture into the paper cases until two-thirds full and bake in the preheated oven for 20–25 minutes, or until light golden and the sponge bounces back when touched. A skewer inserted in the centre should come out clean.
- Leave the cupcakes to cool slightly in the tray before turning out onto a wire cooling rack to cool completely.
- Put the medium marshmallows in a heatproof bowl over a pan of simmering water. Leave until melted and smooth.

- When the cupcakes are cold, hollow out a small
  section in the centre of each one and fill with a
  dollop of melted marshmallow. Leave to cool.
- Stir the mini marshmallows into the vanilla
  frosting by hand until evenly dispersed.
- Spoon the frosting on top of the cupcakes and
  decorate with edible glitter.

Mary Berry's iced fairy cakes recipe

We earn a commission for products purchased through some links in this article.

In this easy iced fairy cakes recipe, Mary Berry makes a batch of 12 simple fairy cakes in just 30 minutes. Each cupcake is topped with a quick icing that is made using two ingredients; icing sugar and warm water. This simple Mary Berry recipe is featured in one of her most famous cookbooks, Mary Berry's Baking Bible.

Ingredients
For The Cake:

- 100 g (4 oz) softened butter
- 100 g (4 oz) caster sugar
- 2 large eggs
- 100 g (4 oz) self-raising flour

- 1 level tsp baking powder

For The Icing:

- 225 g (8 oz) sifted icing sugar
- 2-3tbsp warm water
- handful of sweets, to decorate

Method

- To make this fairy cakes recipe, heat the oven to 200C fan, 180C fan, gas 6. Place fairy cake cases into a 12-hole bun tin, to keep a good even shape as they bake.
- Measure all the ingredients into a large bowl and beat for 2-3 mins until the mixture is well blended and smooth. Fill each paper case with the mixture.
- Bake in the preheated oven for 15-20 minutes until the cakes are well risen and golden brown. Lift the paper cases out of the bun tin and cool the cakes on a wire rack.
- Put the icing sugar in a bowl and gradually blend in the warm water until you have a fairly stiff icing. Spoon over the top of the cakes and decorate with sweets.
- To make orange fairy cakes: Add the grated rind of 1 orange in step 2. To make orange flavoured icing, blend 225 g (8 oz) sifted icing sugar with the juice of 1 orange until you have a fairly stiff icing. Spoon over the tops of the cakes.

Sweetie tray bake

Ingredients
For the cake:
- 200g butter
- 200g caster sugar
- 4 medium eggs
- 200g self-raising flour
- 1tsp baking powder
- Zest of 1 medium orange
- 2-4tsp orange food colouring

To decorate:
- 200g white chocolate
- Smarties, M&Ms, Maltesers, Haribo, Dolly mix, sugar strands, chocolate buttons

Method

- Preheat the oven to 180°C/350°F/Gas Mark 4 and line a small square baking tin (9in x 9in) with greaseproof paper.
- Mix all of the wet ingredients together with an electric hand whisk. Once combined add in the flour, baking powder, orange zest and orange food colouring and mix again.
- The mixture should be smooth and orange in colour. If you're not happy with the colour of your cake mix add in some more food colouring and beat with a wooden spoon.
- Pour the mixture into the tray and bake for 20-25 mins until golden. Turn out onto a wire rack and leave to cool. Once cooled, cut the edges off the bake using a bread knife. This will show off the colour of the sponge inside.
- Place your cake onto your chosen serving plate or board. Next, melt the white chocolate in a microwavable bowl and spoon over the cake and leave to cool.
- Spoon the rest of mixture on top of the cake letting it run down the edges. Giving your cake two coats of white chocolate will make sure there are no crumbs. Leave to cool a little, but not too long as you don't want it to set.
- Cover in different sweets like M&Ms, Smarties, Haribos and leave to set on the side or in the fridge until it's ready to be served.

Chocolate fingers cake recipe

Ingredients
For the cake:
- 200g butter
- 200g caster sugar
- 4 medium eggs
- 150g self-raising flour
- 50g cocoa powder
- ½tsp baking powder

To decorate and fill:
- Nutella
- 3 packs chocolate fingers
- M&Ms, Smarties, Maltesers

Method

- Preheat oven 180C, gas 4. Grease and line 2 x
  20cm cake tins with greaseproof paper. Use the
  all-in-one method to make your sponge; pour
  all of the ingredients into a large mixing bowl
  and whisk with an electric hand whisk until
  combined.
- Once combined, pour into the cake tins making
  sure you they're as even as possible. Bake in the
  oven for 20-25 mins until springy to touch.
- Once baked, turn the cakes out onto a wire rack
  and leave to cool a little. Put the base cake onto
  a serving plate. Spread Nutella over the base
  cake then sandwich the two cakes together.
- Spread the rest of the Nutella over the top of
  the cake using a spatula and spread evenly,
  letting it drip down the sides. Wipe any excess
  chocolate off the plate with a warm wet cloth,
  turning the plate as you go.
- Begin to stick the chocolate fingers around the
  outside, pressing firmly in the middle of each
  chocolate finger so it sticks properly. The trick
  is to let the bottom of the chocolate finger rest
  on the plate and the middle to stick to the cake.
  Leave the cake to one side so the chocolate
  fingers can stick. Meanwhile, decide which
  sweets you're going to use to fill it.
- Scatter the sweets over the cake and pile them
  up until you're happy. Store this cake in the
  fridge until it's ready to be served.

Mary Berry's classic Christmas cake recipe

Ingredients

- 175g (6 oz) raisins
- 350g (12 oz) glace cherries, rinsed, thoroughly dried and quartered
- 500g (1lb 2oz) currants
- 350g (12oz) sultanas
- 150ml (¼ pint) sherry, plus extra for feeding
- Finely grated zest of 2 oranges
- 250g (9oz) butter, softened

- 250g (9oz) light muscovado sugar

- 4 eggs

- 1 tbsp black treacle

- 75g (3oz) blanched almonds, chopped

- 75g (3oz) self-raising flour

- 175g (6oz) plain flour

- 1½ tsp mixed spice

To Finish And Decorate Mary Berry's Christmas Cake You Will Need:

- About 3tbsp apricot jam, sieved and warmed

- Icing sugar

- 675g shop-bought almond paste

- Packet royal icing mix to cover 23cm/9in cake

Method

- Put all the dried fruit in a container, pour over the sherry and stir in the orange zest. Cover with a lid, and leave to soak for 3 days, stirring daily. Grease and line a 23cm (9in) deep round tin with a double layer of greased greaseproof paper. Preheat the oven to 140C, 120C fan, gas 1.

- Measure the butter, sugar, eggs, treacle and almonds into a very large bowl and beat well. Add the flours and mixed spice and mix thoroughly until blended. Stir in the soaked fruit. Spoon into the prepared cake tin and level the surface.

- Bake in the centre of the preheated oven for 4-4½ hours or until the cake feels firm to the touch and is a rich golden brown. Check after 2 hours, and, if the cake is a perfect colour, cover with foil. A skewer inserted into the centre of the cake should come out clean. Leave the cake to cool in the tin.

- When cool, pierce the cake at intervals with a fine skewer and feed with a little extra sherry. Wrap the completely cold cake in a double layer of greaseproof paper and again in foil and store in a cool place for up to 3 months, feeding at intervals with more sherry. (Don't remove the lining paper when storing as this helps to keep the cake moist.)

- Decorate with almond paste and royal icing.

Strawberries and cream cake recipe

Ingredients

- 200g (7oz) butter, softened
- 200g (7oz) caster sugar
- Zest from ½ an orange
- 4 medium eggs
- 200g (7oz) self-raising flour
- 1 level tsp baking powder
- Icing sugar, for dredging

For The Filling And Topping

- 150g (5oz) mascarpone cheese
- 150ml (¼ pint) double or single cream
- 1 tbsp icing sugar
- Zest and juice from ½ an orange
- 2 tbsp good-quality strawberry jam
- 400g (14oz) smallish strawberries

For The Sauce:
- 100g (3½oz) strawberries, roughly chopped
- 1 tbsp icing sugar
- 1 tbsp orange juice
- 2 x 20cm (8in) sandwich tins, buttered and base-lined

Method
- Set the oven to Gas Mark 5 or 190°C. Cream the butter and sugar until light and fluffy. Whisk in the orange zest, then whisk in one egg at a time with 1 tbsp flour each time.
- Add the rest of the flour and the baking powder and 2 tbsp warm water. Mix until smooth. Divide the mixture between the tins, smooth the tops and bake for 25-30 mins until springy to the touch. Cool for 10 mins, then take out of the tins and cool on a wire rack.
- **To make the filling**: Beat the mascarpone with the cream, icing sugar, and orange zest and juice. Spread over the base of one cake and spread the jam over the base of the other cake. Slice the strawberries and arrange two-thirds of them on the creamy cheese filling. Put the other cake on top and press down lightly. Chill.
- **To make the sauce**: Put the berries in a tall jug with the icing sugar and orange juice and whizz to make a sauce to serve with the cake.
- **To serve**: Arrange the rest of the sliced strawberries on top of the cake and dredge with icing sugar. Spoon some sauce over, or, if you prefer, serve separately with the cake.

Salted caramel pretzel brownies recipe

Ingredients

- 150g unsalted butter, plus extra for greasing
- 250g dark chocolate, broken into pieces
- 1tsp instant coffee
- 3 eggs
- 250g golden caster sugar
- 60g plain flour
- 1tbsp cocoa powder

3tbsp Salted Caramel Spread

- 40g salted pretzels
- 1/2tsp sea salt flakes, optional

You Will Need:

- 33cm (13in) x 18cm (7in) tin, lined with parchment

Method

- Preheat the oven to 180C/Gas 4. Melt the butter and chocolate over a bain-marie. Add the instant coffee and 1/2tsp sea salt.
- Whisk the eggs and sugar together until thick and pale. Fold in the melted chocolate mixture. Sift the plain flour and cocoa powder together and fold into the mixture. Put the mixture into the tin. Drizzle over the caramel and use a butter knife to push it through the brownie mixture to create a marbled effect. Tap the tray on the surface.
- Place the pretzels on top. Bake for 30 – 35mins. The brownies will be gooey in the middle but the top should look shiny and cracked. Allow to cool in the tin. Sprinkle over the sea salt flakes. Once cool cut into squares.

Annabel Langbein's ultimate chocolate cake recipe

Ingredients

- 3 cups self-raising flour
- 2 cups sugar
- 1½ tsp vanilla extract
- ¾ cup cocoa powder
- 2 tsp baking soda, sifted
- 200g butter, softened
- 1 cup milk or unsweetened yoghurt
- 3 large eggs
- 1 cup boiling hot coffee

Chocolate Ganache, To Ice

- 500 ml cream

- 500 g best quality dark chocolate, (70% cocoa solids), roughly chopped

- fresh raspberries

Method

- Heat oven to 160°C/325°F. Grease the sides and line the base of a 30cm round cake tin or 2 x 20cm round cake tins with baking paper.

- Place all ingredients except Chocolate Ganache and raspberries in a bowl or food processor and mix or blitz until the ingredients are combined and the butter is fully incorporated.

- Pour mixture into prepared tin or tins and smooth the top.

- Bake for 1 hour or until a skewer inserted into the centre comes out clean. Allow to cool in the cake tin.*

- Pour the cream into a medium saucepan and heat until it is very hot, and almost but not boiling. You'll know it's ready when bubbles start to form around the edge of the pan. Remove from the heat and add the chopped chocolate. Stand for 2 minutes, then stir until the chocolate is fully melted into the cream.

- Whisk this chocolate ganache until it is smooth and glossy, then chill.

- Slather the chilled chocolate ganache over the top of the cake. Top with fresh raspberries and serve.

Simnel cake

Ingredients

- 250g butter, softened
- 250g light soft brown sugar
- 4 medium eggs
- 250g self-raising flour
- 2 level tsp mixed spice
- 250g sultanas
- 125g currants
- 175g glacé cherries
- 125g ready-to-eat dried figs, chopped
- Grated zest of 1 lemon

- Grated zest of 2 oranges

- 2 x 500g packs white marzipan

- 2tbsp ground almonds

- 11 flaked almonds

Method

- To make this Simnel cake, start by setting the oven to cool, Gas Mark 2 or 150°C.
  Put the butter and sugar into a bowl and beat together. Add the eggs, flour and mixed spice alternately and mix well. Add all the fruit and citrus zest and mix again

- Roll out some of the marzipan so that it fits roughly into your cake tin. Put a third of the cake mixture into the tin and spread evenly over the base. Lay your marzipan piece over this mixture.

- Put half of the remaining cake mixture into the tin and lay another marzipan piece on top. Top with the rest of the mixture and level the top. Cook in the centre of the oven for 3-3¼ hrs, until a skewer inserted in the centre comes out clean. Leave the cake to cool in the tin, then remove cake from tin and level the top. Turn the cake over.

- Cut a third off the second block of marzipan and reserve. Roll out the larger piece and lay your cake tin on top of it, cutting the marzipan to fit the size of the cake. Lay the marzipan on top of the cake, and put under the grill to brown slightly.

- Use the reserved marzipan and trimmings to make 11 neat cubes and 11 balls. Roll the balls in the ground almonds.

- Arrange the balls in a circle on top of the cake, using a little water to hold in place. And there you have it, the perfect Easter simnel cake.

The Hummingbird Bakery blueberry cake recipe

Ingredients
For The Cake:
- 350g unsalted butter, at room temperature
- 350g caster sugar
- 6 eggs
- 1tsp vanilla extract
- 450g plain flour
- 2 tbsp plus 2 tsp baking powder
- 280ml soured cream
- 250g fresh blueberries, plus extra to decorate
- 2 quantities cream cheese frosting (see below)
- icing sugar, to decorate
- a 25-cm ring mould, greased and dusted with flour

For The Cream Cheese Frosting:

- 300g icing sugar, sifted
- 50g unsalted butter, at room temperature
- 125g cream cheese, cold
- Makes enough to frost 12 cupcakes (double the recipe for 20-cm cake)

Method

- Preheat the oven to 170°C (325°F) Gas 3.
- Put the butter and sugar in a freestanding electric mixer with a paddle attachment (or use a handheld electric whisk) and cream until light and fluffy. Add the eggs one at a time, mixing well and scraping any unmixed ingredients from the side of the bowl with a rubber spatula after each addition. Beat in the vanilla extract, flour and baking powder until well mixed. Add the soured cream and mix well until everything is combined and the mixture is light and fluffy.
- Gently stir in the blueberries by hand until evenly dispersed.
- Pour the mixture into the prepared ring mould and smooth over with a palette knife. Bake in the preheated oven for 40 minutes, or until golden brown and the sponge bounces back when touched. Leave the cake to cool slightly in the mould before turning out onto a wire cooling rack to cool completely.
- When the cake is cold, put it on a serving plate, cover the top and sides with the cream cheese frosting and decorate with more blueberries. Dust with a light sprinkling of icing sugar.

For the cream cheese frosting:
- Beat the icing sugar and butter together in a freestanding electric mixer with a paddle attachment (or use a handheld electric whisk) on medium-slow speed until the mixture comes together and is well mixed.
- Add the cream cheese in one go and beat until it is completely incorporated. Turn the mixer up to medium-high speed. Continue beating until the frosting is light and fluffy, at least 5 minutes. Do not overbeat, as it can quickly become runny.

Rose and raspberry cake recipe

Ingredients

- 225g golden caster sugar
- 225g unsalted butter, softened
- 4 medium eggs, beaten
- 1 tsp vanilla extract
- 1½ tsp baking powder
- 225g self-raising flour, sifted

For The Rose-Cream Filling:

- 150ml double cream
- 2tsp rosewater
- 4 tbsp raspberry jam
- 150g fresh raspberries

For The Rose Glacé Icing:

- 175g icing sugar
- 2tbsp warm water
- 2tsp rose water

To Decorate:

- Roses
- A handful of fresh raspberries
- Icing sugar, to dust

Method

- Preheat the oven to 180°C/160°C fan/gas mark 4, then lightly butter two cake tins 20cm in diameter and line with baking parchment.
- In a large mixing bowl, beat the sugar and butter together till they are pale and fluffy. Gradually add the beaten egg a little at a time. If the mixture starts to curdle, add a teaspoon of flour and this should bring it back together. Add the vanilla extract. Mix in the baking powder and half the flour, then fold in the rest. Divide the mixture between the cake tins. Smooth the tops, then bake for 20-25 minutes. The cakes should be nicely risen and the sponge should spring back when you press a finger on to it and should have shrunk away slightly from the sides of the tin. Leave the cakes in their tins for 10 minutes before turning out on to a wire cooling rack.
- Meanwhile, whisk the double cream until it stands in soft peaks, adding the rosewater as you go. Then fold in the raspberry jam, being careful not to over-mix, as you want to create a ripple effect.

- When the cakes are completely cool, turn one of them flat base uppermost, slather with the cream mixture and scatter with raspberries, slightly crushed. Top with the second cake. If you've made three cakes, spread more cream and raspberries over the second layer and top with the third.
- For the pink glacé icing, mix together the icing sugar, water and rosewater, and stir in the juice from a few crushed raspberries until it's all looking gloriously pink. Drizzle the rose icing across the cake and don't worry if things are looking a little tipsy. Allow jam, cream, berries and icing to slide if they want to – within reason.
- Arrange the roses, dot with rose petals and the remaining raspberries and dust with icing sugar. If you have any edible silver dust, now's the time. Scatter with silver stars too if you have them, but just a few.
- Finally, cake stand, flutes of Kir Royale or pink lemonade and/or very delicate cups of tea to serve.

Stacie Stewart's skinny carrot meringue cake recipe

Ingredients

- 200ml vegetable oil, plus extra for greasing
- 3 eggs
- 300g soft light brown sugar
- 600g carrots, scrubbed and grated
- 280g self-raising flour
- 1tsp bicarbonate of soda (baking soda)
- 1tsp ground cinnamon
- 1tsp mixed spice (pumpkin pie spice)
- Finely grated zest of 1 orange

- 150g dried fruits, such as cherries, sultanas (golden raisins), raisins (optional)

- 150g nuts, such as pecans or walnuts, toasted and roughly chopped

- Orange-blossom honey, to serve

To Make The Meringue Frosting:

- 6 egg whites

- 300g caster (superfine) sugar

- 1tsp vanilla extract

Method

- Preheat the oven to 180°C/350°F/Gas Mark 4. Grease 2 x 20cm/8in diameter cake tins and line with baking parchment.

- Put the oil, eggs and sugar into a bowl and beat together. Add the carrots and beat until incorporated.

- Sift the flour, bicarbonate of soda and spices into a large bowl. Add the orange zest, dried fruits and nuts and stir to coat them in the flour; this will prevent them from sinking in the cake.

- Add the flour mixture to the carrot mixture in 3 batches, stirring gently after each addition. Divide the mixture between the prepared tins and bake for 40 minutes, or until a skewer comes out clean. Leave to cool in the tins for 10 minutes, then turn out onto a wire rack and leave to cool completely.

- To make the frosting, place a large heatproof bowl over a pan of simmering water, making sure the bottom of the bowl doesn't touch the water. Add the egg whites and sugar and beat with an electric hand whisk until stiff peaks form; this should take about 6 minutes. Remove from the heat, add the vanilla and give it a final few seconds beating. Your frosting will be thick and shiny and must be used right away.

- Place the first cake on a cake board or plate and spread over the meringue frosting – not too much, or it will be pushed out of the sides. Stack the next cake layer on top. Now cover the outside of the cake; I use a palette knife and swipe the frosting up and around the sides, and I think this cake looks better when the frosting isn't smooth. If you're feeling really adventurous, blast the top gently with a blowtorch for a toasted marshmallow effect. Drizzle with a little honey to serve.